WORDPRESS

The Ultimate Solution guide
to build your first Website
and blog from scratch in
just 7 days!

By Wade Diamond

Legal & Disclaimer

The information contained in this book is not designed to replace or take the place of any form of medicine or professional medical advice. The information in this book has been provided for educational and entertainment purposes only.

The information contained in this book has been compiled from sources deemed reliable, and it is accurate to the best of the Author's knowledge; however, the Author cannot guarantee its accuracy and validity and cannot be held liable for any errors or omissions. Changes are periodically made to this book. You must consult your doctor or get professional medical advice before using any of the suggested remedies, techniques, or information in this book.

Upon using the information contained in this book, you agree to hold harmless the Author from and against any damages, costs, and expenses, including any legal fees potentially resulting from the application of any of the information provided by this guide. This disclaimer applies to any damages

Table of Contents

Introduction.....................5

**Day 1: Why WordPress? Deciding that
WordPress is the Best Option**   **6**

What is WordPress?   6

Pros and Cons of WordPress   6

Why You Should Choose WordPress   7

**Day 2: Obtaining a Webhost, Choosing a Name,
and Installing WordPress**   **8**

Choosing a Webhost   8

Choosing a Domain Name   9

Tip About Choosing a Webhost and Domain Name
     10

Installing WordPress   10

Day 3: Choosing a Theme   **12**

Considerations to Make Before Choosing a Theme
     12

Installing Your WordPress Theme   13

Day 4: Adding Pages 14

Types of Pages   14

Creating Your Homepage   14

Custom Menus and Page Attributes   15

Day 5: Adding Posts 16

Choosing Content   16

Understanding SEO   16

Enabling or Disabling Comments   17

Day 6: Using the WordPress Dashboard to Maintain Your Site 18

The WordPress Dashboard   18

Configuring the Dashboard   19

Day 7: Marketing Your WordPress Site   20

Marketing for Businesses   20

Social Media Marketing   21

Update and Post to Your Site Regularly   21

Conclusion   22

Introduction

I want to thank you and congratulate you for downloading my book, *WordPress: The solution guide to build your first website and blog from scratch in just 7 days!* This book is going to teach you everything that you need to know to build your own website from the ground up in just week.

I want to start by saying that this is not a book for technical geniuses. This book is designed for anyone, based on the idea that you do not need thousands of dollars or countless hours of work to build a website. You do not even need the help of a professional- you can build a website yourself, simply by arming yourself with the information found in this book.

At one time, it would be unreasonable for an individual to build their own website. It required knowledge of Flash, CSS, or HTML coding. For most people, these essential parts of web development are hard to grasp. This is especially true if you are busy trying to run your own business and do not have time to learn these skills. Fortunately, content management systems such as WordPress make it possible for anyone to build a website, without the technical knowledge of Flash, CSS, and HTML coding.

In this book, you will find a complete, 7-day guide to completing your own website using WordPress. You will learn why you should use WordPress to build your website, how to set up webhosting, choosing your theme, publishing posts and the importance of SEO, and more.

What are you waiting for? Pick up this book and begin learning what you need to build your website from scratch today.

Good luck and happy reading!

Day 1: Why WordPress? Deciding that WordPress is the Best Option

Are you ready to master WordPress? First, let's discuss what WordPress is and why you should be using it to build your website.

What is WordPress?

WordPress is an open source tool written in PHP coding language that can be used to create blogs, websites, and other types of web content. It is one of the most popular content management systems (CMSs) that is in use today because of its ease of use. This makes it perfect for everyone, even people who have no experience with coding, formatting, creating themes, and the other skills necessary to create a website from scratch.

Pros and Cons of WordPress

Pros

- **WordPress is structured as an open source platform**. This means that programmers that work with WordPress share codes online for use on the site. This makes building your website significantly easier and saves both time and money when it comes to development of your website or blog.

- **WordPress is simple and fast to use.** The WordPress site contains menus and a dashboard that are very simple to use. It allows you to easily build and navigate to the different areas of your site. It is also very easy to install, making setup a breeze.

- **WordPress has plugins that can improve SEO on your site.** If search engine optimization (SEO) has you scratching your head, do not worry. There are a number of plugins available on WordPress that can help improve the SEO on your site without a lot of work.

- **WordPress is very affordable.** WordPress is free to use and install, which is great for users who are looking to set up a basic blog or a business website.

- **WordPress requires less maintenance than building your own site.** When you use WordPress, you can choose to update when necessary. This means that bugs and security holes are fixed without work on your end.

Cons

- **You must rely on WordPress' security**. Unfortunately, because WordPress is open source, its codes are available to everyone online, including hackers. This can make it easier for them to find security holes, though there are a number of measures taken to prevent this from happening.

- **WordPress is not always compatible with larger business or e-commerce sites**. WordPress is perfect if you are a blogger or a small company looking to get the word out about your business. However, it does not have the capacity to handle large businesses or heavy-trafficked e-commerce sites because of its size.

- **WordPress themes are shared among other users**. This means that even when you create your own website, you may end up with a design that is not as unique as you would like. This can have a negative effect on branding in some cases.

Why You Should Choose WordPress

While there are a few disadvantages of working with WordPress, you should keep a few things in mind before you write it off because of a few quirks. First, while it may not be appropriate for larger companies and busy e-commerce websites, WordPress is ideal for small business and blogging websites. It is also very fast, which means that you can quickly get yourself or your business established online. When you combine this with the time and money that you save by choosing WordPress, it is no wonder that it is one of the top choices for building a website.

Day 2: Obtaining a Webhost, Choosing a Name, and Installing WordPress

Now that you have spent time on Day 1 learning about all of the reasons that WordPress is the best option to build your website or blog, it is time to learn how to set up the basics for your website. That is what Day 2 will be about. You will learn how to obtain a webhost, choose a name, and install WordPress.

Choosing a Webhost

WordPress Compatibility

In order for you to use your webhost with WordPress, it is essential that you choose a host that is compatible. While most webhosts will be compatible with content management systems like WordPress, it is a good idea to check and be sure.

The Cost

There are a number of free webhosts out there that will provide a home for your website for free. Unfortunately, this often comes at the cost of ads that clutter your web page and a lack of technical assistance, among other things. Before settling on one of these free hosts, be sure to look for affordable options that offer better benefits for your site at a lower cost.

Something else to keep in mind as you choose which plan to buy (or not to buy) for your site is how they appear to users. Ads and domain names that are not really your own (yoursite.webhost.com) are an indicator of a site that is free. Some users may look at this as inferiority when compared to other sites.

E-Commerce Options

Are you planning on selling products or services online? If so, then it is essential that you choose a webhost that supports this. This often requires a Shopping Cart and an SSL certificate, especially if you are planning on collecting credit card information.

Technical Support

Does the webhost you are choosing offer help when you need it? You may be building your site any time of day and it is important that tech support is there too. In addition to 24/7 technical support, consider response time. A good response time is usually 1-2 hours after a question is asked.

Limits

Some webhosts restrict the amount of web space, PHP, CPU, or bandwidth that your site uses. This can affect how it runs, as well as the number of people that can visit your site at once. Before you sign a contract, be sure that you do not have unreasonable limits that will restrict what you want to do with your website or blog.

Provided Features

What additional features does the webhost offer? Some of the things to consider include a control panel to add and manage accounts, email services, and domain name registration.

Customer Reviews

What are other people saying about the webhost that you are considering? Once you have narrowed down your options to the hosts you may want to work with, do a search to find out information about the webhost. Satisfied customers are the marking of a great webhost.

Choosing a Domain Name

Your domain name is going to be what people type into their address bar to find you. In order for this to happen, you must choose a good domain name. Here are some features of a good domain name to keep in mind before naming your site:

- **A good domain name should be related to your business or blog**. If you are running a business, then your company name makes a great domain name. For a blog, the name of your blog or even your own name may work.

- **Avoid weird extensions**. In previous years, the only options when it came to website endings were .org, .com, .net, .edu, and .gov. Today, there are a number of different extensions, including things like .pizza. Whether you can find a relevant ending or not, stick with something more traditional. Most Internet users are not ready to adapt to weird website endings.

- **Choose a memorable domain name**. In order to choose a memorable domain name, it should be to the point and punchy. You should also try to choose something catchy, to make advertising easier.

- **Remember to choose something you like**. Generally speaking, you will not be able to change your domain name after you have chosen it. Therefore, make sure you choose something that you like- it is going to stick with you through the life of your business or blog.

Tip About Choosing a Webhost and Domain Name

When you are looking for a webhost, be aware that some will provide a free domain name with a paid plan. You may even get a lifetime domain with your plan. While this is a great benefit, you must also consider the possibility that you will want to switch webhosting accounts in the future. If this may happen, then it will be much easier to switch if your hosting account and domain name are not connected.

Installing WordPress

Once you have chosen a webhost, it is time to install WordPress so that you can start building your site.

Step 1: Find Out Your FTP or SSH Information

In order for you to use WordPress with the webhost you have chosen, you need to find your FTP or SSH information, which is the safe file transfer protocol for your chosen host. This will link your WordPress content management system with the webhost that is hosting your domain name.

Step 2: Check Requirements for WordPress

In order to run and install WordPress, it must be compatible with the computer you are working from. Do a quick check to make sure that your computer meets the minimum requirements for the software you are installing.

Step 3: Download WordPress

Go to the WordPress website. You should see an option for downloading the WordPress package. Click the link for download and then unzip all of the files.

Step 4: Create the WordPress Database and Choose a User

Some hosting providers may come with a WordPress database, while others come with an automated set up. You should be able to find out which one you need by checking your webhost's support pages.

If you do need to manually create the database and a user, then follow the set up using the instructions for your specific server. You should be able to access these on your account. When you add the user, make sure that you check the box to allow all privileges.

Step 5: Uploading WordPress Files

Before you start uploading the WordPress files to your webhost, decide whether you want its files to be integrated into the root of your domain or in its own subdirectory in your website. If you want them in the root of your domain, move the unzipped contents of the WordPress into the root directory of the web server you chose. If you want the files in a separate subdirectory (a blog directory, for example), then upload the unzipped files using FTP to the subdirectory of your choice.

Step 6: Access the WordPress URL

To complete the installation, open your web browser and type in address for your site. Accessing it will finish the process.

Congratulations! You have just taken all of the steps to establish your website.

Day 3: Choosing a Theme

On Day 3, you are going to choose the theme for your website. The theme of your website is its appearance. It alters the way that the site is displayed, but does not modify the software that runs the site. It consists of a collection of files that work in conjunction with each other to make a graphical interface and a unified design across an entire website.

Considerations to Make Before Choosing a Theme

The Purpose of Your Website

When choosing a theme, it is important that you choose one that complements the purpose of your site. For example, if you are planning on writing a blog, then you should choose a theme that is easy to read. If the purpose of your site is to sell your product to customers, then you are going to want a theme that allows you to do that.

Compatibility with Other Themes or Plugins

Before you choose a theme, be sure that it is compatible with the plugins that you plan to use on your site. Some themes will not work with certain plugins. Additionally, some themes are hard to change once you choose them. Make sure that you like your theme, or at least that you can change the theme if you are unsure of it.

One plugin that you should be wary of is the multilingual plugin. Some themes will not translate into languages other than English, which can be a huge drawback if you plan to expand your business in the future.

Speed of the Theme

Another factor to consider is how quickly the theme you are choosing will load. Nobody likes slow webpages, not your customers and especially not Google. If your site runs slow, you may also be ranked lower on search page results because of it. Make sure that the theme is not too complex- not all of your customers will be accessing it on a high speed Internet connection.

Mobile Compatibility

In the age of smartphones, consumers can access your site from everywhere. This makes it increasingly important for websites to be accessible to mobile consumers. Some themes will not load on mobile phones, while others require you to adjust the settings so that a different version appears to mobile customers. When your site does adapt to the screen size of a device, it is known as responsiveness. Check for this before selecting the theme for your WordPress site.

Simplicity is Key

It is not uncommon for people unfamiliar with websites and the way that they work to think that flashy layouts are going to grab the eye of your potential readers/customers. While this may be true, simplicity is a far superior angle. Not only will choosing a simplistic design make your site load faster, it will be more usable for customers. Simple layouts are also much more appealing to search engines, which is important for your ranking.

Browser Compatibility

Another thing to consider is whether or not your site works on different browsers. Your site may be accessed from Safari, Google Chrome, Internet Explorer, Firefox, or any other number of browsers. You can do this check manually by accessing your site on these different browsers, or you can find a compatibility test that will check for compatibility against different browsers.

Installing Your WordPress Theme

Step #1: Log in to your administrator account on WordPress and access your dashboard.

Step #2: Click on the "Themes" link. You will find this under the sidebar under the heading "Appearance."

Step #3: Click on the button labeled "Add New" at the top of the themes page. This will direct you to a new screen. Here, you will have the option of choosing a free WordPress theme or uploading a theme that you have purchased from another site.

Step #4: Choose your WordPress theme. Some of the categories that you will see on this page include Popular, Latest, and Featured. You can also search for a specific theme to suit your needs or find a theme that has specific features.

Step #5: Click on your chosen theme and install it to your site. Once you click on a theme, you will be redirected to a preview. There, you will also see a button that says "Install."

Day 4: Adding Pages

A WordPress website consists of many different things, including pages. The pages of your site will be displayed along the top of the homepage or along the side, depending on the theme that you have chosen. Beneath the pages, you can create submenus and add posts.

Types of Pages

There are a number of pages that you may want to add to your site. Be careful of limits based on the theme that you have chosen, especially if you plan on having a lot of pages. Here are some examples of pages you may want to add to your site:

- About Me/ About Us

- Contact

- Testimonies/ Customer Reviews

- Menu

- Locations

- Company Blog

Using Pages to Create Organization for a Blog

Can your blog posts be categorized according to topic? For example, a blog about lower back pain may be organized into categories like Prevention, Managing Your Back Pain, Alternative Remedies, Information, and Back Surgery. A news site may be organized into categories like Local, World News, Politics, Health, and Science & Technology. If the purpose of your site is to publish articles, then you may benefit from breaking your site up into pages according to category.

Creating Your Homepage

If you choose a traditional blog theme, then the homepage of your site will display all of the most recent posts. This can be great if your goal is to attract readers to your website. However, if you are a business, then it may be more beneficial to create a static homepage. This will allow you to display a constant message, such as customer reviews, your location, or whatever other information you would like to display.

Custom Menus and Page Attributes

There is a plugin that you can install called the "Custom Menus" feature. This allows you to nest pages and create submenus, create category pages, change the order of the pages on your site, and add customized links in the navigation menu. If you want this feature, however, it must be compatible with the theme that you have chosen for your website.

If you have a theme that is not compatible with the "Custom Menus" plugin, you would change the order of your pages and set templates and parent pages using the "Page Attributes" area of your dashboard.

Day 5: Adding Posts

The submenus of the pages on your WordPress website are called posts. Whether you are a business or a blog, adding posts can greatly benefit your site. Blogs often post the majority of their content as posts, while businesses may benefit from a company blog or posts about promotions, discounts, and special occasions.

Choosing Content

One of the biggest reasons that companies put off establishing a blog for their site is because they are unsure of what type of posts they should publish. Here are a few tips to help you post great content to your site:

1. **Choose a topic you are passionate about**. Chances are, if you are writing a blog or running a company, then you are already doing something you are passionate about. Continue to do this with your posts, especially if you are writing about something that your customers may be passionate about as well.

2. **Be realistic with your posting goals**. One of the biggest reasons that blogs fail is because unrealistic goals are set for posting. Once you establish a regular schedule for

writing, your readers are going to expect posts. Failing to provide them can make them see you as less reliable, which can be harmful to your blog or business. Therefore, do not expect too much of yourself. Publishing just once or twice a week is more than enough for a blog. Companies may post on their blog even less.

3. **Think about what your customers/readers want to know**. One of the best ways to connect with your readers is to know what they are thinking. Some great questions to ask yourself include:

- How does my business/idea work?

- How does someone get into my field?

- What ideas are related to my area of blogging/business?

- Is there any recent news about my area of interest?

Understanding SEO

Understanding the art of search engine optimization is something that would take books to explain. Here are a few tips for beginners to help you get started:

- **Do not overuse keywords**. Keyword stuffing is a black hat technique that is sometimes used to try to catch the eye of a search engine. However, complex searching algorithms may get your post (or even your entire site) blacklisted from future search engine results.

- **Do use whitespace**. When you use whitespace between the paragraphs of your posts, it makes the reading easier for readers. It also increases readability for search engines, helping you rank higher in results.

- **Take advantage of widgets**. There are a number of WordPress widgets that can help with SEO. Take advantage of these widgets; just make sure they are compatible with your latest WordPress theme.

Enabling or Disabling Comments

On each post, you will also find that you can enable or disable comments. If you are running a blog, or you have a blog section on your company website, then it can be quite beneficial to allow reader comments. This is especially true if you have someone who is going to be managing the site. A comments section allows readers to state how they feel, share the article with friends, and ask further questions about the information you have provided.

Day 6: Using the WordPress Dashboard to Maintain Your Site

One of the great things about WordPress is that you do not have to worry about fixing bugs and technical issues related to the site- you only have to install the latest update. In order to install the latest updates, maintenance your site, add posts, and make changes, you are going to access your WordPress dashboard. This chapter will be all about the dashboard and how to use it.

The WordPress Dashboard

You do not have to poke around your website to access the dashboard area. Just go to the administrator login and put in your username and password. This will redirect you to the dashboard. This section will discuss the main areas.

At a Glance

In the At a Glance section of your administrator dashboard, you will see the number of posts, pages, and comments on your site. This area also displays the theme that is currently running on your website and the spam that has been caught. Additionally, if you click on the comments area, you will be able to load all of the comments without going to the individual pages.

Quick Draft

The quick draft area allows you to choose a title and enter body text, and then saves it as a draft. This is merely a means to allow you to draft your thoughts in a hurry. If you would like to categorize the post or set a future publish date, go to the "Add New Post" screen. This section also provides links to the most recent drafts that you have published, which will redirect you to the area to edit that post.

Activity

The activity area allows you to easily monitor the frequency of your posts, as well as all of the most recent comments. If you hover over a comment, you will see action links including Approve/Unapproved; See the History, Trash, and Mark as Spam, Edit, and Reply. The appropriate form will appear so you can manage the comment on the WordPress dashboard.

Your Stuff

Here, you will find links to all of your own most recent activity, including activity that you have posted on other people's sites. This includes new posts, your most recent comments, and your most recent updates.

What's Hot

In this module, you will find a widget that displays news from Wordpress.com, the top blogs, the top posts, and the latest posts.

Stats

The stats section can be very useful if you are trying to find data on which posts were most effective or when your site was accessed the most. In this area, you will find how much traffic your blog had, as well as links to the most popular areas of your site. You can also click on a specific day for additional details on the traffic for the day.

Configuring the Dashboard

One of the great things about the WordPress dashboard is that you can configure it so that it is displayed how you want. If you want to see your stats displayed before the At a Glance section, you can move the modules. If you do not want to see a section at all, then you can show or hide it. Finally, you can also open and close the different sections directly from the dashboard.

Day 7: Marketing Your WordPress Site

So, is your company website or blog up and running? Great! So, how do you get customers to come to your website? The answer is marketing. In this chapter, we will discuss marketing for businesses, social media marketing, and why you need to update and post to your site regularly.

Marketing for Businesses

If you own a business, then having a website can be very beneficial in attracting new customers and encouraging growth. In order for it to be helpful, follow these tips to help market your business:

1. **Have a company blog**. While establishing a website is a huge step toward business success, having a blog section can be just as important. This is true for a number of reasons, including:

    - People looking for information on the content you are posting may be redirected to your site. This can raise the number of clicks to your website.

    - Having credible information on your company blog raises your credibility and your level of expertise with your customers.

- A blog shows interest and passion in your area, which is important to customers.

2. **Advertise on other business materials**. Do you have pens or business cards advertising your phone number or address? You can also use these to advertise your website.

3. **Think like your customers**. Do you envision your customers as working adults who listen to the radio every day or teenagers who keep their noses buried in their phones? Knowing who to reach out to about your business and how is essential for reaching the right customers. Think about how your audience is most likely to see your message and advertise it in that way.

4. **Always track your efforts**. Pay close attention to how you spend money advertising and its effectiveness. In order to further track your efforts, consider setting up links that take you to the home landing page but track where you clicked them from. This will give you an idea of how potential customers are finding you.

Social Media Marketing

Whether you are a business or a blog, it is essential that you connect with customers on social media. Some of the best sites for social media marketing include Facebook, Twitter, Instagram, Pinterest, Google+, YouTube, LinkedIn, and Tumblr. Here are a few tips to keep in mind as you market your business on social media.

1. **Sync your social media accounts**. You can save yourself a lot of time and effort by syncing your social media accounts so that they all update when one is updated. For example, if you post to the company blog, sync it so that your other social media accounts broadcast the new post.

2. **Choose your 5 or fewer accounts based on your audience**. You may have better success contacting other professionals on sites like LinkedIn and Google+, while you may be better able to reach out to teenagers on sites like Tumblr and Instagram. You should not have more than 5 social media accounts (even five is difficult for a full-time employee to manage), so make your selections carefully.

3. **Hire somebody especially for social media marketing**. Social media marketing can be a

full time job, especially if you are working on more than one site. If you cannot dedicate yourself to this, make sure that you hire someone who can.

4. **Know the best times to post**. Knowing when your audience is going to be accessing social media can be extremely beneficial for marketing. Do your research and make the majority of your posts when you know your readers are going to be online.

5. **Use images**. Users are significantly more likely to read a post with an eye-catching image than one without. Use images that are relevant to your article and attractive to the eye to get the most out of your social media posts.

Update and Post to Your Site Regularly

Have you ever come across a website that clearly has not been updated in a long time? Chances are, unless you are very specific with your search results, you do not see these websites. The reason for this is that search engines like Google are known to list WordPress sites higher or lower based on their activity. The good news is that this reduces some of the work that you have to do, because WordPress broadcasts your posts and additions using SEO keywords every time that you make an addition to your site.

Conclusion

What do all great WordPress sites have in common? They were created by people who know what they are doing. Fortunately, it is so simple that you can arm yourself with the knowledge found in this book and complete your own website in just one week.

Whether you are a blogger or a small business owner, this book should have taught you all that you need to know to build your site from the ground up. Here is a quick re-cap of a few of the things that you have learned.

1. The reasons that WordPress is one of the top content management systems

2. How to choose a domain name and webhost

3. How to install WordPress and choose a theme

4. How to publish pages and posts

5. How to use the WordPress dashboard

6. How to market and maintain your website

Armed with these bits of knowledge, you should now feel confident enough to build your own site.

Whether you are a blogger or a small business owner, best of luck in your future website endeavors!

Wade Diamond

Check Out Other Books

Go here to check out other related books that might interest you: